✝

Growing Pains
Don't Stop Your Purpose

✝

"ALL THINGS WORK TOGETHER FOR YOUR GOOD"

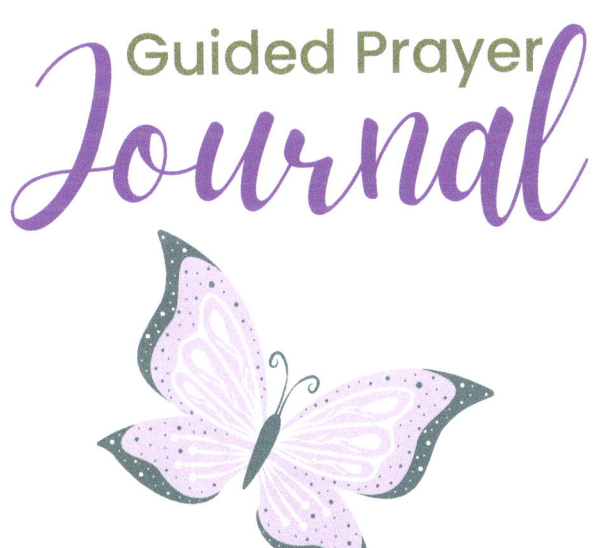

Guided Prayer
Journal

"BE STILL AND KNOW THAT I AM GOD."
— PSALM 46:10

Yolanda Russell Upshaw

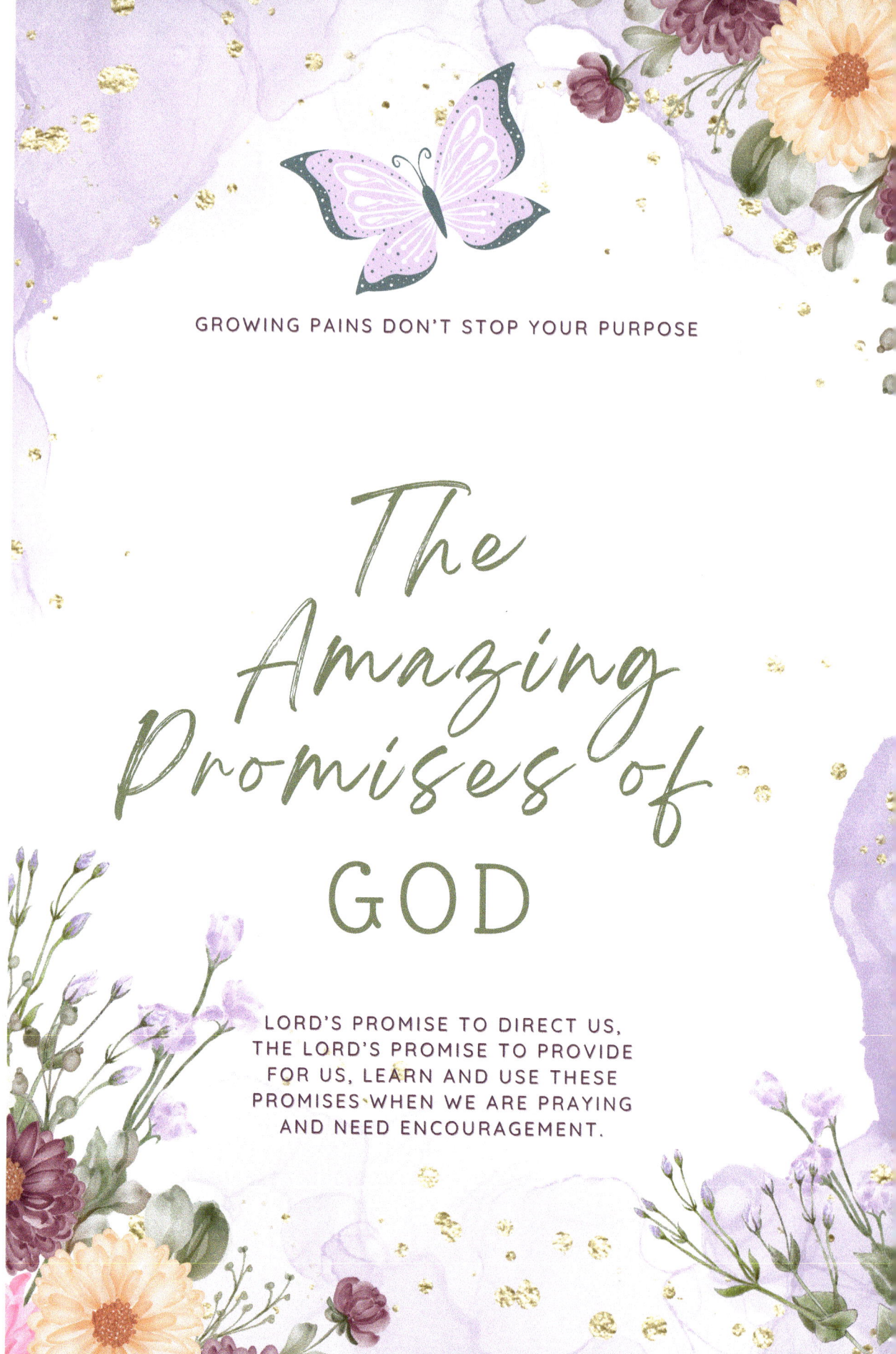

GROWING PAINS DON'T STOP YOUR PURPOSE

The Amazing Promises of GOD

LORD'S PROMISE TO DIRECT US, THE LORD'S PROMISE TO PROVIDE FOR US, LEARN AND USE THESE PROMISES WHEN WE ARE PRAYING AND NEED ENCOURAGEMENT.

ISBN: 979-8-9923903-1-5

Published by: JLAW Publishing

Printed in the United States of America

Scripture quotations are taken from the Holy Bible, New

International Version (NIV), unless otherwise noted.

Introduction

Life often brings us challenges we never anticipated and struggles we feel unprepared to face. As I reflect on my own journey, I've come to realize that these "growing pains" were never meant to stop me but to mold and prepare me for God's greater purpose. From the heartache of childhood abandonment to navigating broken relationships, from the deep ache of being motherless to the profound joy of becoming a mother myself, every chapter of my life has been intertwined with pain but also covered by God's undeniable grace.

This guided prayer journal is more than a retelling of my story. It's a space for you to pause, connect with God, and discover how prayer can bring healing, hope, and strength no matter where you find yourself. Prayer became my anchor during turbulent seasons, and it's through prayer that I experienced peace, purpose, and the promises of God in my life.

As you turn these pages, I encourage you to open your heart to the transformative power of prayer. Together, we'll explore how prayer aligns us with God's will, connects us to His promises, and brings clarity and peace even in life's most difficult moments. No matter what you're facing, remember this: God is always at work, using even the hardest seasons to shape you for His purpose. Let this journal be your companion on the path to healing, renewal, and a deeper relationship with the One who holds your story.

Who is this book for?

This book is for anyone who feels broken but longs for healing. It's for the single mother trying to make ends meet, the woman recovering from trauma, the man seeking reconciliation with his family, and the believer longing for a deeper relationship with God. It's for anyone who has ever felt abandoned, rejected, or stuck and is ready to experience the peace and purpose that only God can provide.

No matter where you are on your journey, this book will guide you to see how prayer is not just a lifeline but a powerful tool for transformation.

Preface

Prayer has been the cornerstone of my life, the unbreakable thread that has connected me to God through every trial, every triumph, and every moment in between. As I reflect on my journey, I now see how His hand was always at work, even when I couldn't feel or understand it. In the moments of silence, when I questioned whether He was near, God was faithfully orchestrating a plan far greater than I could imagine.

This book is a labor of love, a heartfelt offering born out of the lessons I've learned through seasons of pain and the profound peace I've found in the presence of God. Each page reflects my journey of resilience, faith, and surrender, showing how prayer has not only carried me but transformed me.

It is my deepest prayer that as you turn these pages, you will be inspired to draw closer to God, to pray with boldness and authenticity, and to trust Him even when the path seems unclear. May this journal remind you that God is always at work, weaving the threads of your life into a beautiful tapestry of purpose and grace. Trust that He is working all things together for your good. Let this be the start, or renewal, of a powerful prayer journey that changes everything.

With love and faith,
Yolanda R. Upshaw

Forward

In a world where pain sometimes can overshadow purpose, Yolanda R. Upshaw shines as a beacon of hope and a living testimony that God's grace is truly sufficient. Her journey within this journal is one of resilience, transformation, and unwavering faith. I have had the privilege of witnessing Yolanda's journey firsthand, and I can confidently say that she is a woman whose life has been molded by the power of prayer and the promises of God.

This guided prayer journal is not just an ordinary journal but a testament of her life guided and strengthen through by God word and prayer; it is also an invitation to step into a sacred space where healing begins, faith is renewed, and purpose is discovered. Yolanda courageously opens her heart, sharing her personal experiences with honesty and transparency. Through her words, she offers more than just encouragement, she provides practical tools for prayer, self-reflection, and spiritual growth.

What makes this journal extraordinary is Yolanda's ability to connect with reality and the reality of her readers. Her authenticity and heartfelt wisdom transcend the pages, reminding us that God can take the shattered pieces of our lives and create something beautiful. Her journey is a testament to the truth found in Romans 8:28: "And we know that in all things God works for the good of those who love Him, who have been called according to His purpose."

Forward

As you navigate this journal, you'll be inspired to pray boldly, reflect deeply, and trust God with every area of your life. Whether you are walking through a season of brokenness, seeking clarity in your purpose, or longing for a deeper relationship with God, this journal is a companion that will guide you toward hope and healing.

Yolanda's story is more than a testimony, it's a ministry birthed from her faith and the lessons she has learned through life's challenges. Her life proves that pain is not the end of the story; it's often the beginning of something greater. I encourage you to embrace this journey with an open heart, knowing that God has a unique purpose for you as well.

Let this journal be a tool to strengthen your prayer life, align your heart with God's will, and remind you that even in the darkest moments, His light is always shining. Be prepared to be challenged, uplifted, and transformed as you embark on this journey with Yolanda as your guide.

Dr. Joy Riley

Founder and Editor in Chief of Younspire Magazine Author | Speaker | Advocate for Purpose-Driven Living

Dedication

This book is lovingly dedicated to my children: Curtis, Tosheka, Jolanda, and Cheryl. You are the light of my life, and I love you more than words can ever express.

To my grandchildren: G-ma love you all unconditionally.

To my siblings, uncles, aunties, nieces, nephews, family, and friends, each of you has played a meaningful role in my journey. In one way or another, you have shaped my story, supported me, and enriched my life. I love you all deeply and am forever grateful for your presence in my life.

To my parents Curtis and Lottie Russell, may you rest in peace and forever watch over our family. It was your love and sacrifices that gave me the gift of life, I cherish the memories of you and miss you every single day. The lessons you taught me, both in your presence and your absence, have profoundly shaped who I am today. Through every high and low, God has worked it all together for my good, and I thank Him for the foundation you laid.

With all my love, Yolanda R. Upshaw

Table of Contents

Growing Pains Don't Stop Your Purpose

Prayer played a vital role in my foundation that held my life together. My life was a paradox of brokenness and promise. I was born into a world where love was present but fractured, a world where my parents' struggles often overshadowed their hopes for me. My birth wasn't just the start of my life; it was the beginning of a spiritual journey that God was already shaping. As a child, I felt the weight of separation when my parents' relationship crumbled, leaving me torn between

two worlds. The confusion of being pulled in opposite directions brought deep pain, and I often questioned why I couldn't have the family I longed for. When my mother eventually left, her absence created a void that felt overwhelming. I wrestled with feelings of abandonment, questioning my worth and craving the love and security I so desperately needed. In those early years, prayer became my lifeline, even when I didn't fully understand its power. In the stillness of the night, I whispered words to a God I barely knew, hoping He was listening. Little did I know that those quiet prayers would become the foundation of my peace and strength. God's presence was a constant, unseen hand steadying me when I thought I couldn't stand.

When I moved in with my father, my life took a different turn. He wasn't perfect, but in his own way, he stepped into the gap left by my mother's absence, teaching me about love, protection, and resilience. Through him, I glimpsed the heart of my Heavenly Father.

Growing Pains Don't Stop Your Purpose

My father's lessons about hard work, faith, and perseverance became the bedrock of the woman I would grow to be.

Still, the ache of a motherless childhood lingered. I longed for her presence, her guidance, and her nurturing touch. But even in her absence, God was planting seeds of purpose in my life. When I became a mother myself, I was determined to break the cycle. I prayed over my children, asking God to guide me where I lacked experience, and He faithfully answered. Without a blueprint, I leaned on His wisdom, and His grace covered my shortcomings.

Even in the midst of all, I thank God for reconciliation that in time, my mom and I reunited, and she moved back into the place in which we all once lived.

The brokenness of my family rippled through my life, affecting my relationships, my choices, and even how I saw myself. Yet, through the cracks, God's light began to shine, revealing a greater purpose in the pain. There were moments when giving up seemed like the best option, when despair whispered lies that I wasn't enough. But God's Spirit within me kept pushing, whispering that my story wasn't over.

In the midst of breakthroughs, a breakthrough happened. It wasn't a dramatic moment; it was the quiet realization that God had been with me all along, using every trial to prepare me for a purpose far greater than I could imagine.

Growing Pains Don't Stop Your Purpose

Even when I tried to navigate life without Him, when rejection, sickness, and growing pains clouded my vision, His grace never left me. Healing came when I committed to prayer and fasting, when I surrendered my wounds to God and allowed Him to transform them into something beautiful. Through forgiveness and letting go of the past, I discovered the peace and purpose that only He can provide. Each painful step of my journey prepared me for the ministry, community work, and calling that now define my life.

This journey isn't just mine; it's a testimony of God's faithfulness and the power of prayer. It's a reminder that growing pains don't stop your purpose, they refine it. Through every tear, every prayer, and every triumph, I've seen how God works all things together for good. My prayer is that as you walk through your own journey, you'll discover that same truth: God's plans for you are greater than any pain you'll endure, and His peace will carry you through.

How Prayer Grounds Us

Prayer is the foundation of a relationship with God. It grounds us in His presence and provides the strength to face life's challenges. As I look back over the years of my life, I can see so clearly how prayer became my lifeline a thread that connected me to God even in my moments of deepest pain, separation, and abandonment. When my parents' relationship fell apart and I was caught in the middle, I didn't have the words to articulate the confusion and heartbreak I felt. Yet, in those moments, I found myself whispering prayers, not fully understanding their power but somehow knowing they were being heard.

Key Scripture:

"Before I formed you in the womb I knew you, before you were born I set you apart." – Jeremiah 1:5

"The Lord is close to the brokenhearted and saves those who are crushed in spirit." – Psalm 34:18

Practical Tips:

1. Establish a daily prayer routine, even if it's only five minutes.
2. Write down your prayers to reflect on God's answers over time.
3. Start your prayers with gratitude to set your heart in the right posture.

How Prayer Grounds Us

Journal Questions:

1. What are moments in your life where you felt abandoned, and how did you see God work through these situations?

   _____

   _____

   _____

   _____

   _____

   _____

2. What specific areas of your life can you surrender to God today through prayer?

   _____

   _____

   _____

   _____

   _____

   _____

Recipe of Prayer:

- Gratitude: Begin by thanking God for His presence and blessings.
- Confession: Share your struggles and ask for His forgiveness.
- Supplication: Bring your needs and desires before Him.
- Listening: Spend time in silence to hear His voice.

A Father's Love How Prayer Reveals God's Heart

Prayer allows us to experience the love of our Heavenly Father, even when earthly relationships fall short. My earthly father's love mirrors the care and provision God offers us.

Key Scripture:

- "See what great love the Father has lavished on us, that we should be called children of God!" – 1 John 3:1
- "The Lord your God is with you, the Mighty Warrior who saves. He will take great delight in you; in his love he will no longer rebuke you but will rejoice over you with singing." Zephaniah 3:17

Practical Tips:

1. Speak to God as a loving Father during prayer, not as a distant deity.
2. Reflect on moments when God showed His love and provision.
3. Keep a gratitude journal to document His faithfulness.

Journal Questions

1. How has God shown His love and provision for you during difficult times?_____

_____

2. What areas of your heart need to experience the love of God as your Heavenly Father?_____

_____

The Feeling of a Motherless Child

Growing up without the presence of my mother in my life at the time, left an undeniable void. There were moments I felt incomplete, longing for love and guidance I believed only a mother could provide. The absence felt like a constant reminder of what I didn't have a nurturing embrace, comforting words, and the assurance that someone was there to teach me how to navigate life. Mother's Day became a painful reminder of what was missing, and I often asked God, "Why me?"

For those who feel this way, I want you to know that you are not alone. While the absence of a mother can leave scars, God has a way of stepping in to fill those empty spaces. He becomes the ultimate nurturer, the parent who never leaves, the comforter who wipes every tear. He hears the cries of the motherless and offers a love so profound that it can heal even the deepest wounds.

God's Word reminds us that He is a loving parent to us all. Psalm 27:10 says, "Though my father and mother forsake me, the Lord will receive me." This verse became an anchor for me when I felt abandoned. It reminded me that God's love is unfailing, even when human love falls short.

The Feeling of a Motherless Child

Another comforting scripture is Isaiah 66:13: "As a mother comforts her child, so will I comfort you." God's promise to comfort us is not just words it is a living, breathing reality for those who lean on Him. I found that in the quiet moments of prayer, God's presence became my solace. His love whispered to me that I was not forgotten, and His hands carried me through every challenge I faced.

If you are feeling the weight of being motherless, take heart. God is with you, guiding and loving you in ways that surpass human understanding. Lean into His love and let Him fill the spaces where you feel broken.

 The Feeling of a Motherless Child How Prayer Fills the Gaps When we feel a void in life, prayer bridges the gap and fills us with God's

nurturing presence. My experience of growing up without my mother in my teens, reminds us that God provides everything we need.

Key Scriptures for Encouragement:

- Psalm 27:10: "Though my father and mother forsake me, the Lord will receive me."
- Isaiah 66:13: "As a mother comforts her child, so will I comfort you." Matthew 11:28: "Come to me, all you who are weary and burdened, and I will give you rest."
- Psalm 34:18: "The Lord is close to the brokenhearted and saves those who are crushed in spirit."

The Feeling of a Motherless Child

Practical Tips:

1. Turn your feelings of lack into prayers for God's provision.

2. Seek God's wisdom and guidance when navigating new roles, such as parenthood.

3. Use the Psalms as a guide for expressing your emotions to God.

Journal Questions:

1. What voids have you felt in your life and how has God filled them?

_____

_____

_____

2. What does it mean to you that God is both a Father and a comforter?

_____

_____

_____

A Prayer for the Motherless

Heavenly Father, I come to You feeling the weight of what is missing in my life. I long for the love and guidance that I never received from my mother. But Lord, Your Word promises that You will never leave me or forsake me. Be my comforter, my guide, and my strength. Fill the empty spaces in my heart with Your unfailing love. Help me to trust in Your plan for my life and to find peace in Your presence. In Jesus' name, Amen.

Results of a Broken Family: How Prayer Heals Brokenness

Brokenness within a family leaves wounds that can feel impossible to heal. When a family fractures whether through divorce, abandonment, or unresolved conflict it can create ripple effects of pain, mistrust, and feelings of inadequacy. I know this feeling well. My own family's challenges often left me questioning my worth and struggling to understand why things had to be so hard. The broken pieces of my family became the backdrop of my life story, but through those cracks, God's light began to shine.

Prayer became the bridge that connected my brokenness to God's restoration. I discovered that prayer isn't just about asking God to fix the situation it's about inviting Him into the hurt and allowing Him to heal from the inside out. Through prayer, I learned to forgive, to let go of bitterness, and to trust God with the pieces I couldn't put back together myself. He showed me that even in the midst of brokenness, there is hope.

One of the most comforting scriptures during my journey was Psalm 147:3: "He heals the brokenhearted and binds up their wounds." It reminded me that God specializes in mending what feels shattered beyond repair. He doesn't just patch up the cracks; He creates something new, something stronger, something beautiful.

Results of a Broken Family: How Prayer Heals Brokenness

Another scripture that carried me through was Isaiah 61:3, where God promises to give us "a crown of beauty instead of ashes, the oil of joy instead of mourning, and a garment of praise instead of a spirit of despair." These words reminded me that my pain wasn't the end of the story God was working behind the scenes to bring restoration and joy.

If you're facing the effects of a broken family, I want to encourage you to bring it to God in prayer. Be honest with Him about your pain, your anger, and your questions. Ask Him to give you a heart of forgiveness and to heal the wounds that feel too deep to touch. Trust that God's plan for your life is not derailed by the brokenness in your family He can use it to shape you, strengthen you, and prepare you for His purpose.

Results of a Broken Family How Prayer Heals Brokenness:
Prayer invites God into the broken areas of our lives, where He can bring
healing and restoration. My family challenges were the backdrop for God's redeeming work.

Results of a Broken Family: How Prayer Heals Brokenness

Practical Steps for Healing Brokenness Through Prayer:

1.Acknowledge the Pain: Be honest with yourself and God about the hurt you feel. Healing begins with acknowledgment.

2.Forgive Daily: Forgiveness is not a one-time event, it's a process.

3.Ask God to help you forgive, even when it feels impossible.

4.Pray for Your Family: Intercede for each family member, asking God to work in their lives and bring restoration where it's needed.

5.Let Go of Control: Trust that God's timing is perfect and release the need to fix everything on your own.

6.Focus on God's Promises: Meditate on scriptures about healing, restoration, and God's unfailing love.

Journal Q&A:

1.How can you be a vessel of God's peace in your family dynamics?_____

2.Are there family members you struggle to forgive? What steps can you take to begin the process of forgiveness?

_____

_____

3.How have you seen God's hand at work in your family, even in the midst of brokenness?_____

4.What scripture or promise from God brings you the most comfort during this time?_____

Results of a Broken Family: How Prayer Heals Brokenness

Key Scriptures for Healing Brokenness:

·Psalm 147:3: "He heals the brokenhearted and binds up their wounds."

·Isaiah 61:3: "To bestow on them a crown of beauty instead of ashes, the oil of joy instead of mourning, and a garment of praise instead of a spirit of despair."

·Romans 8:28: "And we know that in all things God works for the good of those who love Him, who have been called according to His purpose."

·Colossians 3:13: "Bear with each other and forgive one another if any of you has a grievance against someone. Forgive as the Lord forgave you."

·2 Corinthians 5:18: "All this is from God, who reconciled us to himself through Christ and gave us the ministry of reconciliation."

God's healing power is greater than any brokenness you may feel. When you invite Him into the wounds of your family, He can transform the pain into something beautiful. You are not defined by the brokenness around you.

God is working to create a story of redemption and restoration in your life. Trust Him with every piece.

Results of a Broken Family: How Prayer Heals Brokenness

A Prayer for Healing Family Brokenness

Heavenly Father, you see the pain and brokenness within my family. I feel the weight of it, but I trust that You are a God of healing and restoration. Help me to forgive where forgiveness is needed and to release the bitterness that has taken root in my heart. Lord, bring peace to the areas of conflict and restore the bonds that have been broken. Heal the wounds in each of our hearts and let Your love bring unity where there is division. Thank You for working all things together for good, even when I can't see it yet. In Jesus' name, Amen.

Giving up was never an option

Life has a way of pressing us into corners where giving up seems like the only option. The weight of trials, disappointments, and unanswered prayers can leave us feeling drained, questioning our ability to keep moving forward. I've had my share of valley moments in those dark places where I felt utterly alone, overwhelmed, and ready to throw in the towel. But it was in those very moments, when I thought I had no strength left, that God met me in prayer and renewed my spirit.

Prayer became my lifeline when I felt like I was sinking. It wasn't about saying the perfect words; it was about being honest with God, crying out in frustration, fear, and exhaustion. Through prayer, I learned that I didn't have to carry the weight of my struggles alone. God reminded me of His promise in Isaiah 40:31: "But those who hope in the Lord will renew their strength. They will soar on wings like eagles; they will run and not grow weary; they will walk and not be faint."

There were times when I sat in prayer and could barely whisper, "Lord, help me." Yet, even in those small prayers, His presence brought comfort. I didn't always feel immediate relief, but over time, I realized that every moment spent in His presence gave me the strength to take another step. He reminded me through His Word that His grace is sufficient, and His power is made perfect in my weakness (2 Corinthians 12:9).

Giving up was never an option

When you feel like giving up, remember this: You don't have to rely on your own strength. God's Spirit within you empowers you to keep going. Philippians 4:13 says, "I can do all things through Christ who strengthens me." This isn't just a verse to memorize, it's a truth to cling to in the hardest moments. Prayer connects you to the limitless strength of God, allowing you to press forward even when you feel empty.

Desire to Give Up How Prayer Renews Strength:
When life feels overwhelming, prayer renews our strength and helps us press forward. My valley moments remind us that God's Spirit empowers us to keep going.

Key Scripture:
- "But those who hope in the Lord will renew their strength." – Isaiah 40:31
- "My grace is sufficient for you, for my power is made perfect in weakness." 2 Corinthians 12:9

Practical Steps to Renew Strength Through Prayer:

1.Be Honest with God: Don't hold back your emotions. Let God know exactly how you feel, He can handle your frustrations and fears.

2.Meditate on His Promises: Spend time reading and declaring scriptures about God's strength and faithfulness. Write them down and bring them with you.

3.Pray for Strength Daily: Begin each day by asking God for the strength to face whatever lies ahead.

4.Rest in His Presence: Sometimes the best prayer is silence. Sit quietly and allow God's peace to renew your heart and mind.

5.Keep a Gratitude List: Reflect on how God has helped you through tough times in the past. Gratitude shifts your focus from despair to hope.

Journal Q&A:

1.What challenges make you feel like giving up? How can you invite God into them?_____

_____

_____

_____

2.How has God renewed your strength in the past?

_____

_____

_____

_____

_____

3.Reflect on a time when God gave you strength to overcome something difficult._____

_____

_____

_____

_____

4.How did it shape your faith?_____

_____

_____

_____

5.What promises from scripture bring you the most comfort and encouragement when life feels overwhelming? _____

_____

_____

_____

_____

6.How can you remind yourself daily that God's strength is greater than your struggles?_____

_____

_____

_____

_____

_____

Giving up was never an option

Key Scriptures for Strength and Perseverance:

- Isaiah 40:31: "But those who hope in the Lord will renew their strength. They will soar on wings like eagles; they will run and not grow weary; they will walk and not be faint."
- 2 Corinthians 12:9: "My grace is sufficient for you, for my power is made perfect in weakness."
- Philippians 4:13: "I can do all things through Christ who strengthens me."
- Psalm 46:1: "God is our refuge and strength, an ever-present help in trouble."
- Matthew 11:28-29: "Come to me, all you who are weary and burdened, and I will give you rest. Take my yoke upon you and learn from me, for I am gentle and humble in heart, and you will find rest for your souls."

Giving up was never an option

When the desire to give up feels overwhelming, remember that God's strength is made perfect in your weakness. Prayer isn't just a way to survive, it's a way to thrive in the face of adversity. No matter how heavy the burden feels, God's Spirit within you will empower you to keep pressing forward. You are not alone, and with Him, you can do all things.

A Prayer for Renewed Strength:

Heavenly Father, I come to You feeling weary and overwhelmed. Life feels too heavy, and I don't know if I have the strength to keep going. But Lord, Your Word promises that those who wait on You will renew their strength. Help me to trust in Your power when I feel weak. Remind me that Your grace is sufficient and that You are with me in every step. Fill me with Your Spirit, renew my hope, and give me the courage to keep moving forward. Thank You for being my refuge and strength, my ever-present help in times of trouble. In Jesus' name, Amen.

.

The Breakthrough
How Prayer Opens Doors

Breakthroughs often come when we least expect them, right in the midst of our brokenness. When life feels shattered, and we think there's no way out, prayer becomes the key that opens doors we didn't even know existed. My story is a testament to this truth. In the darkest moments, when I felt lost, forgotten, and overwhelmed by life's challenges, prayer was the light that guided me toward breakthrough.

Prayers have a way of shifting the atmosphere. It moves us from focusing on our problems to fixing our eyes on God's promises. In those moments of prayer, I learned to stop asking "why" and start trusting "how", how God was going to use my pain, my setbacks, and my tears for His glory. I discovered that breakthroughs often require us to let go of our own plans and align ourselves with God's will. As Proverbs 3:5-6 reminds us: "Trust in the Lord with all your heart and lean not on your own understanding; in all your ways submit to Him, and He will make your paths straight."

In one of the most broken seasons of my life, I cried out to God, not knowing how things would change. Through prayer, God didn't just mend the broken pieces. He transformed them into something greater. That's the power of a breakthrough: it's not about returning to what was but stepping into something new, something better. Isaiah 43:19 says, "See, I am doing a new thing! Now it springs up; do you not perceive it? I am making a way in the wilderness and streams in the wasteland."

The Breakthrough
How Prayer Opens Doors

Prayer is where we align ourselves with God's power. It's not about demanding answers but about surrendering our hearts. When we let go of control, God opens doors no man can shut (Revelation 3:8). He clears paths through the wilderness, provides streams in the desert, and makes the impossible possible. Breakthroughs are not about our timing; they're about His perfect plan.

Breakthroughs often come in the midst of brokenness. My story shows how prayer ushers in God's power and aligns us with His will.

Key Scriptures for Breakthrough:

·Isaiah 43:19: "See, I am doing a new thing! Now it springs up; do you not perceive it? I am making a way in the wilderness and streams in the wasteland."

·Revelation 3:8: "See, I have placed before you an open door that no one can shut."

·Proverbs 3:5-6: "Trust in the Lord with all your heart and lean not on your own understanding; in all your ways submit to Him, and He will make your paths straight."

·Ephesians 3:20: "Now to Him who is able to do immeasurably more than all we ask or imagine, according to His power that is at work within us."

·Luke 18:1: "Then Jesus told His disciples a parable to show them that they should always pray and not give up."

The Breakthrough
How Prayer Opens Doors

·Practical Steps to Pray for a Breakthrough:

- ·Be Persistent: Keep praying, even when it feels like nothing is happening. Breakthroughs often come after seasons of perseverance (Luke 18:1-8).

- ·Surrender Completely: Release your plans, fears, and desires to God. Pray for His will to be done above all else.

- ·Listen and Obey: Spend time listening to God's voice and be ready to act in faith when He leads.

- Pray Boldly: Ask God to move in ways beyond what you can imagine. Ephesians 3:20 reminds us that He can do immeasurably more than we ask or think.

- ·Thank Him in Advance: Thank God for the breakthrough before it happens, trusting that He is already at work.

Breakthroughs are a demonstration of God's power and faithfulness. They remind us that no situation is too far gone for His redemption. Whatever brokenness you may face, know that through prayer, God can open doors, restore hope, and lead you into a new season. Trust Him, keep praying, and get ready to see Him move. Your breakthrough is on the way!

The Breakthrough
How Prayer Opens Doors

Journal Questions

1.What breakthrough are you praying for in this season?

_____

_____

_____

_____

2.How can you align your heart with God's will as you wait?

_____

_____

_____

_____

3.What areas of your life feel broken or stagnant? How can you

bring these to God in prayer?_____

_____

_____

_____

4.Have you experienced a breakthrough before? How did

prayer play a role in that moment?

_____

_____

_____

5.What does it mean for you to align your heart with God's

will?_____

6.What specific breakthroughs are you asking God for today?

_____

_____

The Breakthrough
How Prayer Opens Doors

A Prayer for Breakthrough:

Father God, I come to You feeling broken and unsure of the next step. But Lord, I trust that You are the God of breakthroughs, the One who opens doors that no one can shut. I surrender my plans and ask for Your will to be done in my life. Align my heart with Yours and help me to see the ways You are working, even in the midst of my challenges. Thank You for making a way in the wilderness and streams in the wasteland. I believe in Your power to do the impossible, and I thank You in advance for the breakthrough that is coming. In Jesus' name, Amen.

-

Life's Journey Prepares You for Your Purpose

How Prayer Aligns You with God's Plan

Life often feels like a winding road, filled with unexpected detours, delays, and challenges. At times, it's hard to see how pain, struggles, and setbacks fit into any greater plan. But through prayer, I've learned that every trial is a steppingstone toward the purpose God has designed for me. My trials weren't wasted, they were preparation. They shaped me, refined me, and aligned me with the calling God had placed on my life long before I understood it.

Prayer is the bridge that connects us to God's plan. It's in those quiet moments with Him that we gain clarity, strength, and direction. When I didn't know which way to turn, prayer became my compass. Through prayer, God reminded me of His promise in Jeremiah 29:11: "For I know the plans I have for you," declares the Lord, "plans to prosper you and not to harm you, plans to give you hope and a future."

Looking back, I can see how every difficulty served a purpose. The pain I endured gave me compassion for others. The challenges I faced taught me resilience and trust. The moments of waiting strengthened my faith in God's timing. Every season, good and bad, was part of His process to prepare me for what He called me to do. Romans 8:28 assures us: "And we know that in all things God works for the good of those who love Him, who have been called according to His purpose."

Life's Journey Prepares You for Your Purpose

Prayer not only reveals our purpose, but it also aligns our hearts with God's will. It shifts our focus from what we want to do, to what He wants for us. It teaches us to trust His timing, His methods, and His promises. Through prayer, we can embrace the journey, knowing that even our trials are tools in God's hands to shape us for His glory.

Prayer reveals and prepares us for our purpose. My trials became steppingstones to my calling. If you're in a season of uncertainty, take heart. God is using every part of your journey, every success, every setback, every tear, to prepare you for something greater. Prayer is your connection to His plan, the tool that aligns your heart with His purpose. Trust that He is working, even when you can't see it. Your trials are not wasted; they are the building blocks of the amazing future God has in store for you. Keep praying, keep trusting, and step boldly into the purpose He's calling you to.

Key Scriptures for Trusting God's Plan:

- ·Jeremiah 29:11: "For I know the plans I have for you," declares the Lord, "plans to prosper you and not to harm you, plans to give you hope and a future."
- ·Romans 8:28: "And we know that in all things God works for the good of those who love Him, who have been called according to His purpose."

Life's Journey Prepares You for Your Purpose

- ·Proverbs 19:21: "Many are the plans in a person's heart, but it is the Lord's purpose that prevails."

- ·Proverbs 3:5-6: "Trust in the Lord with all your heart and lean not on your own understanding; in all your ways submit to Him, and He will make your paths straight."

- ·Psalm 138:8: "The Lord will fulfill His purpose for me; Your steadfast love, O Lord, endures forever."

Life's Journey Prepares You for Your Purpose

Journal Q&A:

1. What trials or challenges in your life have shaped you the most? How can you see God's hand at work in those experiences

_____

_____

_____

2. Are there areas where you're struggling to trust God's plan? How can you surrender those to Him in prayer?

_____

_____

_____

3. What steps can you take to align your daily life with God's purpose for you? _____

_____

_____

_____

4. How has God used a past struggle to prepare you for something greater? _____

_____

_____

_____

_____

Life's Journey Prepares You for Your Purpose

Practical Steps to Align with God's Plan Through Prayer:

1. Pray for Clarity: Ask God to reveal the purpose behind your trials and how He's using them to prepare you.

2. Surrender Your Plans: Release your desires and ambitions to God, trusting that His plan is better than anything you could imagine.

3. Seek His Will Daily: Make it a habit to ask, "Lord, what would You have me do today?" and trust Him to guide your steps.

4. Reflect on Past Victories: Look back on how God has already worked through your life's challenges, and let it strengthen your faith for the future.

5. Be Patient in the Process: Trust that preparation takes time, and God's timing is always perfect.

A Prayer for Alignment with God's Purpose:

Father God, I thank You that my life is in Your hands and that You have a plan for me. Help me to trust that everything I've been through is preparing me for the purpose You've designed for my life. Lord, align my heart with Your will and help me to see my trials as steppingstones to something greater. Teach me to surrender my plans and to trust Your timing. Reveal the next steps I should take and give me the strength to walk in obedience. Thank You for working all things together for my good and for Your glory. In Jesus' name, Amen

The Power of Prayer Brings Reconciliation

Reconciliation is a reflection of God's redemptive work in our lives. Even when relationships seem irreparably broken, the power of prayer can restore what was lost. Allow my testament of reuniting with my mother is a testament to how God answers prayers in His timing, mending hearts and rebuilding bonds. This chapter emphasizes the transformative power of prayer in mending relationships, reminding you that no relationship is beyond God's ability to heal and restore. It's a call to trust Him with the broken pieces and believe that His redemptive work will bring peace and reconciliation in His perfect time.

Key Scripture References:

·"All this is from God, who reconciled us to himself through Christ and

·gave us the ministry of reconciliation." 2 Corinthians 5:18

·"Bear with each other and forgive one another if any of you has a grievance against someone. Forgive as the Lord forgave you." Colossians 3:13

·"If it is possible, as far as it depends on you, live at peace with everyone." Romans 12:18

·"Blessed are the peacemakers, for they will be called children of God." Matthew 5:9

The Power of Prayer Brings Reconciliation

- The Role of Prayer in Reconciliation: Reconciliation begins in the heart. Prayer allows us to surrender our pain, resentment, and pride to God, inviting Him to heal the brokenness within us and in our relationships. As we pray, God works in ways we cannot see, softening hearts and opening doors for restoration.

- God's Timing is Perfect: Reconciliation with my mother didn't happen overnight. It came in God's perfect timing, showing that while we may want instant results, true reconciliation often requires patience, growth, and spiritual maturity.

- Forgiveness as a Foundation for Reconciliation: Forgiveness is not just for the other person; it frees us from the burden of bitterness. By forgiving my mother, it created a space for God's healing power to flow. Forgiveness doesn't excuse the hurt but acknowledges God's ability to transform and redeem.

- Praying for Restoration: When relationships are strained, it can feel easier to avoid the pain than to face it. Prayer equips us with the courage to seek peace, the wisdom to discern when to speak, and the grace to let God lead.

The Power of Prayer Brings Reconciliation

Practical Points for Application:

- ·Pray Specifically for Reconciliation: Bring the relationship to God in prayer. Name the person, the pain, and the hope you have for restoration. Ask for His will to be done in both hearts.

- ·Release Control to God: Understand that reconciliation is a two-way process. While you can't control the other person's response, you can trust God to work in His timing.

- ·Take Steps Toward Peace: After praying, be open to opportunities to extend an olive branch. This could be a call, a letter, or simply a kind gesture. Let God guide your actions.

- ·Practice Gratitude for Small Steps: Reconciliation may come in stages. Celebrate the small victories a conversation, a shared moment, or an act of kindness and trust that God is working.

The Power of Prayer Brings Reconciliation

Journal Questions:

1. Who in your life needs reconciliation, and how can you begin praying for that relationship today?_____

_____

_____

2. Are there areas where unforgiveness is blocking your ability to reconcile? How can you release this to God in prayer? _____

_____

_____

_____

3. What steps can you take this week to extend peace or forgiveness to someone in your life? _____

_____

_____

_____

4. Reflect on a time when God reconciled a relationship in your life. How did prayer play a role in that process?

_____

_____

_____

_____

The Power of Prayer Brings Reconciliation

Recipe of Reconciliation through Prayer:

1. Confess the Hurt: Acknowledge the pain to God honestly.

2. Forgive: Release the burden of bitterness to make room for healing.

3. Intercede: Pray for the person and ask for God's blessing over them.

4. Seek Peace: Be open to God's direction on how to take the first step.

5. Trust: Leave the outcome in God's hands. knowing He is faithful.

Prayer for Reconciliation:

"Heavenly Father, thank You for being a God of reconciliation. You have restored us to Yourself through Christ, and I ask that You bring that same restoration to my relationship with [name]. Soften both of our hearts and guide us in forgiveness and understanding. Help me to release any resentment and trust Your perfect timing. May Your peace rule in our hearts and Your love bridge the gap between us. In Jesus' name, Amen."

This book
belongs to

Daily Powerful Prayers

IN THE LAST ROW ADD YOUR FAVE PORWERFUL PRAYER VERSES

SUN	MON	TUE	WED	THU	FRI	SAT
PROTECTION PSALM 91:14	HEART PROVERBS 4:23	ETERNAL SECURITY JOHN 3:16	OBEDIENCE EXODUS 20:12	RELATION-SHIPS PSALM 133:1	FRIENDSHIPS PROVERBS 17:17	HEALTH PROVERBS 3:7-9
EDUCATION PROVERBS 1:5	GIFTS AND TALENTS 1 COR 12:4-5	PURITY PSALM 119:9	COURAGE 1 JOHN 4:18	MINDS ROMANS 12:2	INFLUENCES PROVERBS 13:20	SPOUSE EPHESIANS 5:24- 27
DISCERNMENT PSALM 11 9:125	FORGIVE-NESS MATTHEW 6:14	PURPOSE ROMANS 8:28	AGAINST STRONG-HOLDS 2 COR 10:4	GUIDANCE PROVERBS 1:5	FAITH HEBREWS 11:1	CALLING 2 THESSA-LONIANS 1:11
AGAINST SEXUAL TEMPTATIONS 1 COR 10:13	HEART PROVERBS 4:23	THEIR FUTURE JEREMIAH 29:11	UNDERS-TANDING PROVERBS 3:1-3	THEIR SELF-IMAGE ISAIAH 43:1	DECISIONS PROVERBS 3:5-6	DILIGENCE PROVERBS 12:24
MARRIAGE HEBREWS 13:4	FAMILY GALATIANS 6:10	LEADERSHIP PROVERBS 11:30	DESIRES PSALM 37:4	PEACE PHILIPPIANS 4:6-7	WISDOM JAMES 1:5	LOVE MATTHEW 22:37

Notes:_____

_____

_____

_____

_____

37

NOTES

Date: _____

NOTES

Date: _____

NOTES

Date: _____

NOTES

Date: _____

NOTES

Date: _____

_____

_____

_____

_____

_____

_____

_____

_____

_____

_____

_____

_____

_____

_____

_____

_____

_____

_____

_____

_____

_____

IMPORTANT NOTES

January	February	March

April	May	Jun

July	August	September

October	November	December

NOTES

Date: _____

_____

_____

_____

_____

_____

_____

_____

_____

_____

_____

_____

_____

_____

_____

_____

_____

_____

_____

_____

For I know the plans I have for you, declares the Lord, plans for welfare and not for evil, to give you a future and a hope.

JEREMIAH 29:11

Reflection

DATE:

REFLECT ON HOW THE PROMISE APPLIES TO YOUR LIFE, SITUATIONS, OR CHALLENGES. WRITE DOWN YOUR THOUGHTS, EMOTIONS, AND INSIGHTS.

And we know that in all things God works for the good of those who love him, who have been called according to his purpose.

ROMANS 8:28

Reflection

DATE:

REFLECT ON HOW THE PROMISE
APPLIES TO YOUR LIFE,
SITUATIONS, OR CHALLENGES.
WRITE DOWN YOUR THOUGHTS,
EMOTIONS, AND INSIGHTS.

Fear not, for I am with you; be not dismayed, for I am your God; I will strengthen you, I will help you, I will uphold you with my righteous right hand.

ISAIAH 41:10

Reflection

REFLECT ON HOW THE PROMISE
APPLIES TO YOUR LIFE,
SITUATIONS, OR CHALLENGES.
WRITE DOWN YOUR THOUGHTS,
EMOTIONS, AND INSIGHTS.

The Lord is my shepherd; I shall not want.

PSALM 23:1

Reflection

REFLECT ON HOW THE PROMISE
APPLIES TO YOUR LIFE,
SITUATIONS, OR CHALLENGES.
WRITE DOWN YOUR THOUGHTS,
EMOTIONS, AND INSIGHTS.

Come to me,
all you who are
weary and
burdened, and I
will
give you
rest.

MATTHEW 11:28-30

Reflection

DATE:

REFLECT ON HOW THE PROMISE
APPLIES TO YOUR LIFE,
SITUATIONS, OR CHALLENGES.
WRITE DOWN YOUR THOUGHTS,
EMOTIONS, AND INSIGHTS.

And my God will meet all your needs according to the riches of his glory in Christ Jesus.

PHILIPPIANS 4:19

Reflection

DATE:

REFLECT ON HOW THE PROMISE APPLIES TO YOUR LIFE, SITUATIONS, OR CHALLENGES. WRITE DOWN YOUR THOUGHTS, EMOTIONS, AND INSIGHTS.

Because he loves me," says the Lord, "I will rescue him; I will protect him, for he acknowledges my name. He will call on me, and I will answer him; I will be with him in trouble, I will deliver him and honor him.

PSALM 91:14-15

Reflection

REFLECT ON HOW THE PROMISE
APPLIES TO YOUR LIFE,
SITUATIONS, OR CHALLENGES.
WRITE DOWN YOUR THOUGHTS,
EMOTIONS, AND INSIGHTS.

But those who hope in the Lord will renew their strength. They will soar on wings like eagles; they will run and not grow weary, they will walk and not be faint.

ISAIAH 40:31

Reflection

DATE:

REFLECT ON HOW THE PROMISE APPLIES TO YOUR LIFE, SITUATIONS, OR CHALLENGES. WRITE DOWN YOUR THOUGHTS, EMOTIONS, AND INSIGHTS.

But seek first
his kingdom
and
his
righteousness,
and
all these things
will be given to
you as well.

MATTHEW 6:33

Reflection

DATE:

REFLECT ON HOW THE PROMISE
APPLIES TO YOUR LIFE,
SITUATIONS, OR CHALLENGES.
WRITE DOWN YOUR THOUGHTS,
EMOTIONS, AND INSIGHTS.

For no matter how many promises God has made, they are 'Yes' in Christ. And so through him the 'Amen' is spoken by us to the glory of God.

2 CORINTHIANS 1:20

Reflection

REFLECT ON HOW THE PROMISE
APPLIES TO YOUR LIFE,
SITUATIONS, OR CHALLENGES.
WRITE DOWN YOUR THOUGHTS,
EMOTIONS, AND INSIGHTS.

*God
is our refuge
and
strength,
an ever-present
help in
trouble.*

PSALM 46:1

Reflection

REFLECT ON HOW THE PROMISE APPLIES TO YOUR LIFE, SITUATIONS, OR CHALLENGES. WRITE DOWN YOUR THOUGHTS, EMOTIONS, AND INSIGHTS.

10 Minute Devotionals

3 STEPS FOR TURNING SCRIPTURE INTO PRAYER

1. Pick Your Passage.
2. Read Your Passage.
3. Pray Your Passage.

Begin like you would a normal prayer. (Dear Father, Dear Jesus, Oh Lord, etc.) If you are writing out your prayer, treat it like writing a letter. Answer the following question: What command do I see? Ask God for help in obedience. What aspects of God's character are revealed? Praise Him for Who He is. What is God doing? Give Him thanks for His good works. What sin does it reveal in your heart? Confess it in your prayer.

PSALM 23:1-3

_____
_____
_____

2 CORINTHIANS 12:9-10

_____
_____
_____

JOSHUA 1:9

_____
_____
_____

JAMES 1:5-8

_____
_____
_____

JAN

S	M	T	W	T	F	S
			1	2	3	4
5	6	7	8	9	10	11
12	13	14	15	16	17	18
19	20	21	22	23	24	25
26	27	28	29	30	31	

FEB

S	M	T	W	T	F	S
						1
2	3	4	5	6	7	8
9	10	11	12	13	14	15
16	17	18	19	20	21	22
23	24	25	26	27	28	

MAR

S	M	T	W	T	F	S
						1
2	3	4	5	6	7	8
9	10	11	12	13	14	15
16	17	18	19	20	21	22
23	24	25	26	27	28	29
30	31					

APR

S	M	T	W	T	F	S
		1	2	3	4	5
6	7	8	9	10	11	12
13	14	15	16	17	18	19
20	21	22	23	24	25	26
27	28	29	30			

MAY

S	M	T	W	T	F	S
				1	2	3
4	5	6	7	8	9	10
11	12	13	14	15	16	17
18	19	20	21	22	23	24
25	26	27	28	29	30	31

JUN

S	M	T	W	T	F	S
1	2	3	4	5	6	7
8	9	10	11	12	13	14
15	16	17	18	19	20	21
22	23	24	25	26	27	28
29	30					

JUL

S	M	T	W	T	F	S
		1	2	3	4	5
6	7	8	9	10	11	12
13	14	15	16	17	18	19
20	21	22	23	24	25	26
27	28	29	30	31		

AUG

S	M	T	W	T	F	S
					1	2
3	4	5	6	7	8	9
10	11	12	13	14	15	16
17	18	19	20	21	22	23
24	25	26	27	28	29	30
31						

SEP

S	M	T	W	T	F	S
	1	2	3	4	5	6
7	8	9	10	11	12	13
14	15	16	17	18	19	20
21	22	23	24	25	26	27
28	29	30				

OCT

S	M	T	W	T	F	S
			1	2	3	4
5	6	7	8	9	10	11
12	13	14	15	16	17	18
19	20	21	22	23	24	25
26	27	28	29	30	31	

NOV

S	M	T	W	T	F	S
						1
2	3	4	5	6	7	8
9	10	11	12	13	14	15
16	17	18	19	20	21	22
23	24	25	26	27	28	29
30						

DEC

S	M	T	W	T	F	S
	1	2	3	4	5	6
7	8	9	10	11	12	13
14	15	16	17	18	19	20
21	22	23	24	25	26	27
28	29	30	31			

JAN

S	M	T	W	T	F	S
				1	2	3
4	5	6	7	8	9	10
11	12	13	14	15	16	17
18	19	20	21	22	23	24
25	26	27	28	29	30	31

FEB

S	M	T	W	T	F	S
1	2	3	4	5	6	7
8	9	10	11	12	13	14
15	16	17	18	19	20	21
22	23	24	25	26	27	28

MAR

S	M	T	W	T	F	S
1	2	3	4	5	6	7
8	9	10	11	12	13	14
15	16	17	18	19	20	21
22	23	24	25	26	27	28
29	30	31				

APR

S	M	T	W	T	F	S
		1	2	3	4	
5	6	7	8	9	10	11
12	13	14	15	16	17	18
19	20	21	22	23	24	25
26	27	28	29	30		

MAY

S	M	T	W	T	F	S
					1	2
3	4	5	6	7	8	9
10	11	12	13	14	15	16
17	18	19	20	21	22	23
24	25	26	27	28	29	30
31						

JUN

S	M	T	W	T	F	S
	1	2	3	4	5	6
7	8	9	10	11	12	13
14	15	16	17	18	19	20
21	22	23	24	25	26	27
28	29	30				

JUL

S	M	T	W	T	F	S
		1	2	3	4	
5	6	7	8	9	10	11
12	13	14	15	16	17	18
19	20	21	22	23	24	25
26	27	28	29	30	31	

AUG

S	M	T	W	T	F	S
						1
2	3	4	5	6	7	8
9	10	11	12	13	14	15
16	17	18	19	20	21	22
23	24	25	26	27	28	29
30	31					

SEP

S	M	T	W	T	F	S
		1	2	3	4	5
6	7	8	9	10	11	12
13	14	15	16	17	18	19
20	21	22	23	24	25	26
27	28	29	30			

OCT

S	M	T	W	T	F	S
				1	2	3
4	5	6	7	8	9	10
11	12	13	14	15	16	17
18	19	20	21	22	23	24
25	26	27	28	29	30	31

NOV

S	M	T	W	T	F	S
1	2	3	4	5	6	7
8	9	10	11	12	13	14
15	16	17	18	19	20	21
22	23	24	25	26	27	28
29	30					

DEC

S	M	T	W	T	F	S
		1	2	3	4	5
6	7	8	9	10	11	12
13	14	15	16	17	18	19
20	21	22	23	24	25	26
27	28	29	30	31		